The Research Paper Guide

by Anthony C. Sherman

Edited by Robert B. Ewald

PENDULUM PRESS, INC., West Haven, Connecticut 06516

Dedicated to all who use this book.
May you have diligence and patience,
and may you find your reward.

ISBN 0-88301-020-4

Published by
Pendulum Press, Inc.
The Academic Building
Saw Mill Road
West Haven, Connecticut 06516

Printed in the United States of America

Cover design and illustrations by Roland Rodegast

CONTENTS

ABOUT THE AUTHOR

Anthony C. Sherman is a Phi Beta Kappa graduate of Hampden-Sydney College in Virginia. As a recipient of a Rockefeller Fellowship, he received his B. D. and S. T. M. degrees from Yale University. After two years at the College of William and Mary, he became chairman of the social science department and was responsible for curriculum development at Foote School in New Haven, Connecticut.

ABOUT THE EDITOR

Robert B. Ewald is currently a bibliographer for the Library of Congress. A graduate of Hampden-Sydney College, Ewald received his M. S. degree in library science from Simmons College in Boston and a degree in theology from Harvard University. For two years, Ewald served as a bibliographer for a book publishing firm in Germany.

A few years ago, the assignment of a research paper was the concern of the college freshman. Now, most high school students and even junior high students have to write research papers. This downward push of academic expectations presents problems for students. They have not had adequate experience in the procedures required to write papers when research assignments are made. This book is written for the student faced with writing the research paper.

An organized approach to research, documentation, and composition will make the task easier. To provide an approach and methodology for research writing is a function of *The Research Paper Guide*.

It has also been designed as a handbook of techniques and a reference of the documentary forms required to write a paper properly. Examples of many forms in documentation have been included to assist the student. The examples, however, also serve another function. They have been chosen to stimulate ideas for suitable research paper topics.

The forms of documentation used in the book follow the

conventions recommended in the second edition of the *MLA Style Sheet,* published by the Modern Language Association of America.

A word of appreciation is in order for Bonnie Sherman, who skillfully employed encouragement and chastisement, a combination only a wife can master.

—Anthony C. Sherman

CHAPTER I

Introduction

"If only I knew then what I know now!" That's the lament of many students when they hand in their research papers. Why? Learning the procedures for research takes valuable time. But you only learn research procedures by writing papers. This manual will help you with procedures so you may spend your time more fruitfully on research and writing.

Let's begin with what you know about research now. Think about it for a moment. You have done research and lots of it. How do you keep up with the music scene, the style changes for the coming season, or the latest in sports? You do basic research. Your favorite radio station keeps you informed about the top hits and the new releases. Magazines like *Seventeen* and close observation of "those in the know" tell you what's in fashion. The sports page of the newspaper and broadcast reports keep you abreast of the sports world.

Furthermore, you've made reports to others about your findings. You automatically sort out information and pass it on to your friends.

Research, then, is not new or foreign to you. You do it

constantly. But in a research paper, you've been asked to apply these skills differently and in a new form. Your teacher wants you to do research in a specific area; to gather materials, primarily through reading; and to put your findings and conclusions on paper.

There are a number of ways to make the experience enjoyable. To choose a topic that interests you is most important. Don't be trapped by that old line—"I'm going to write on such-and-such because there's a book on it in the library." Your teacher can be helpful in finding a topic suitable for you. He too wants you to find the experience worthwhile and enjoyable. Finally, give yourself plenty of time. You have a month or so from the announcement of the paper to its due date. Get to work on it immediately. Few of life's experiences are worse than a one-night-stand research paper. Don't take our word for it; ask a college freshman.

Why write a research paper?

Your teacher isn't interested in just keeping you busy for the next two months or forcing you to burn the midnight oil. He is trying to help you develop skills which will serve you well throughout your life.

How? Research assignments will become routine aspects of your later high school and college life. That you are learning the basics now is excellent. If you enter the business or professional world, the process learned in writing research papers will be invaluable.

There are also immediate rewards. Do you know how to use a library? Or is it just a room full of books? By writing a research paper, you will learn how to use a library. This ability alone makes the project worthwhile. Information about the Beatles, facts to win the best-car argument, the history of space exploration—all can be found in a library.

Perhaps most important to you, writing a research paper can be fun. Many students have been surprised to discover they enjoyed writing a paper. It brings a feeling of fulfillment—to see, hold, and feel a small volume that you have created. You will know more about your topic than your classmates, your parents, and perhaps, even the teacher. And nothing is more rewarding for a teacher than to be taught by his students.

What is a research paper?

A research paper is a presentation of what others have to say on a given subject (a report), and it may also include your own conclusions (an evaluation). Such a paper has two functions: (1) it informs the reader about a particular subject and provides him with easy access to the sources used (a bibliography) and specific references to these sources (footnotes) and (2) it demonstrates to the instructor that you have mastered the skills required in research methods, documentation, and composition. Initially, the second function will be of equal importance to the first in the evaluation of your paper. In later years, however, the primary function of a research paper will be to provide information and additional sources for the reader in a specific area of study.

What steps are involved in writing a research paper?

The steps involved in writing a research paper are the same, regardless of the subject and the academic area in which the paper has been assigned. These procedural steps are logical and orderly. They must follow one from the other. You simply cannot write a paper without proper research, good notes, and a clear outline of what is to be covered in the paper. This cannot be emphasized too strongly. Students get into difficulties because they do not allow sufficient time to do each step thoroughly.

Writing a research paper requires time, perhaps several months to write a 1000–2000 word paper. Set up a time schedule for each step and stick to it. In this way, you won't have to rush or be overcome with that final week panic. Get to work early. It will be rewarding. The steps in planning and carrying out a research paper are simple and uncomplicated:

1.   Topic. Select a topic that interests you and con-forms to the limits specified by your teacher.

2.   Preliminary outline. Jot down the main ideas you feel must be included in a paper on this topic. In some instances, it will be necessary to complete general reading on the topic before your outline can be prepared.

3.   Bibliography. Make a list of all the sources you may be able to use for your topic.

4.   Reading and taking notes. Read your sources carefully and with discrimination; take clear, accurate notes.

5.   Revision of preliminary outline. Revise your pre-liminary outline in light of your reading and notes.

6.   First draft. Write a rough draft with the idea of putting your points and ideas on paper. Don't worry (at this point) about grammar, punctuation, and spelling.

7.   Revision of rough draft. Revise your paper with attention to style and transitions, and then mechanics —grammar, punctuation, and spelling.

8.   Documentation. Set up your footnotes according to the final revision of your paper and write your bibliography.

9.   Final copy. Write the paper you plan to hand in; make it your best.

10.   Proofreading. In your final reading, look for all possible errors.

On the inside back cover of this book, you will find a checklist of instruction specifications you need from your teacher. It will help you make sure you have the necessary information to write the paper according to his requirements.

CHAPTER II

Topic and outline

Choosing the right topic.

Generally speaking, a teacher allows a certain degree of freedom in picking a topic. He wants you to be able to write about a subject that interests you because this is important in writing a good paper. If you're not interested in your topic, rest assured that your reader won't be either. To stimulate your own interest, choose a topic which will increase your knowledge. If you feel you are knowledgeable in a particular field, perhaps you should not write in this area.

For example, your hobby is keeping up with the latest developments in space exploration. A paper on the history of space exploration may not be the best for you. Why? You may be bored with the research. Reading authoritative sources won't reveal much that is new. Thus, you will lack sufficient motivation to do the research thoroughly.

On the other hand, let's assume you are also interested in the Beatles. You like their music, but you don't know much about them or their sudden rise to stardom. A paper on the Beatles would be an ideal topic for your research paper.

Choose a topic that interests you. Choose a topic from which you will learn.

A word of caution should be added about the scope of your topic. Don't pick a topic that is so broad you cannot possibly handle it within the word or page limit prescribed by the teacher. Let's say you have chosen your topic. It's the "American Civil War." And you have a limit of 12 pages. That topic is far too big and general to handle in 12 pages.

On the other hand, don't choose a topic that is too specific or limited. Your library may not be extensive enough to give you adequate resource materials. "The Social Life of Gideon Wells During the Civil War" would strain the resources of most libraries.

But let's suppose you're still interested in writing a paper on some aspect of the Civil War. "Why Meade Won at Gettysburg" or "Lee's Defeat at Gettysburg" might interest you. Are you intrigued? Are library resources sufficient? Does it meet the qualifications of the assignment? If you can answer *yes* to these questions, you've made a good topic choice.

Frequently, once he begins his research, a student discovers his topic is too broad. If this happens to you, restrict the scope of the paper even further. Limit the size and range of the subject to make it fit the requirements. Let us once again assume you're writing about the Civil War. That's too big, so let's limit it to "Lee and the Army of Northern Virginia." After doing some general reading in the library, you discover this topic is still too much for the requirements. Then, be more specific. What about *one battle* of Lee's Army of Northern Virginia in the American Civil War? "Lee's Defeat at Gettysburg" might do the trick.

This reduction process—starting with an idea of writing

a paper on the Civil War and reducing it until you decide to write on "Lee's Defeat at Gettysburg"—is what we mean by restricting or limiting the scope of your paper.

If you cannot state the idea of your paper in one sentence, then you probably have not narrowed the scope of your paper sufficiently.

Outline

There will be frequent references in this book to the outline, its importance, and use. But just what is an outline? An outline is a map of your paper. It gives you direction in research and writing. It gives the reader a clear framework of what you are saying in the paper.

An outline is not a separate part in research procedure, but something you should keep in mind throughout the process of writing a paper. You will have at least two distinct outlines of your research paper: a preliminary outline and a final outline. Between these two, may be many more. This is the way it should be.

Your first outline will change during your research and even during the writing. An outline will constantly grow, alter, and diminish. What you originally considered a major section may become a subdivision. A subdivision may develop into a separate unit. Or you may discover one section should precede another. The necessity of new sections, not in your preliminary outline, is a possibility as well. Don't be chained by your original outline; let it develop as you read and write.

Preliminary outline

After you have chosen the topic for your paper, make an

outline of what you intend to do. What do you want to say? What are you going to cover in this paper? What are the important points to be developed? Such questions directed at your topic will get you started.

Don't worry about what has been left out or whether it follows logically. A preliminary outline is a rough sketch to give you direction in ideas and possible research sources. The following is an example of a rough outline.

The Beatles: How and Why They Reached the Top

Background: Is there anything there, besides the usual (birthdays, education, and jobs), that contributes to their music and style?

Formation of Beatles: How did they get together?

The big break: How did it happen? Who helped?

Public reaction: What was the reaction in England, abroad (particularly, America)?

Analysis of their music:
Music heritage—styles that helped shape the Beatles.
Lyrics—speak to youth.
Appearance—distinctive hair and dress.
Publicity—dependence on above, yet more.
Influence—"spin-off" groups, styles, and later music.

Once you have completed a rough outline, you will want to set it up in a formal outline style. You are, no doubt, familiar with conventional outline forms:

        I.
        II.
            A.
            B.
                1.
                2.
                    a.
                    b.

   Several points may refresh your memory about outlin-
ing. (1) Indentation is a means of showing importance in
an outline. Headings on the same margin are of approximately equal value. (2) Each heading should be a noun or
noun equivalent (gerund or infinitive phrase). Don't use
"To the top" as a heading, but "Rising to the top" or
"Rise to fame." (3) A single division is incorrect. Nothing
divides into only one part:

   (Correct)   (Incorrect)
   A. Beatle background.   A. Beatle background.
      1. Birth information.   1. Birthdays.
      2. Education.
      3. Jobs.
   The following is a preliminary outline set up according to
conventional outline form.

The Beatles: Their Success and Why
I. Background of the Beatles
  A. Biographical data
  B. Education
  C. Jobs
  D. Events that shaped the Beatles
II. Formation of the Beatles
III. Their big break
IV. Public reaction
  A. England
  B. Abroad (particularly America)
V. Analysis of their success
  A. Music heritage
  B. Lyrics
  C. Appearance
  D. Publicity
  E. Influence

If you have picked a topic you know little about, you may have to do general reading before you write a preliminary outline. This predicament is not uncommon. Some students, just as a general rule, prefer to skim books, encyclopedias, magazines, and newspaper articles before they write their preliminary outline. If this is your situation, by all means, do this general reading first, but with a particular point in mind—writing your preliminary outline.

Once you have selected a topic that fits the requirements set by the teacher (have him review your topic if you are in doubt) and have written a rough outline, then you are ready for what many consider the most exciting part of being a student: the research. Some people find it so rewarding that they make a career of it—professors and research specialists. Who knows, you may find a vocation in writing your paper.

CHAPTER III

Finding research sources

Your next step is to find resources for your paper. You need a working bibliography, a list of possible sources—books, magazine and newspaper articles, and other sources that relate to the topic. Seeking good sources for a bibliography is like a treasure hunt or being a detective on the trail of a suspect. It is fun but you have to be alert and thorough. Your best source may be the one you're too tired to find or dismiss with, "I have enough materials."

The primary source for materials is the library: the one in school, the public library, or a nearby college library, if you are permitted to use it.

Regardless of size, shape, or location—all libraries have the same features. Familiarity with your library and its layout will prepare you for any library.

The fundamental units of a library should be familiar:

1. The card catalogue. The card catalogue is situated in a conspicuous place, generally in the main reading area. It contains a list of all books in alphabetical order that are in that library. The card catalogue is a bibliography of the library. It is the most important place for you in seeking resource materials.

2. Stack area. Circulating books (ones that may be

19

checked out) are placed on open shelves. This section is called the stacks.

3. Reference section. Some books do not circulate because constant use requires they remain in the library. These books are found in the reference area. Books in this category would include: almanacs, atlases, books of quotations, dictionaries, encyclopedias, indexes, periodicals, year books, and others the library feels are important enough to be restricted. This area will be invaluable for bibliographical sources.

4. Reserve area. Books on reserve, that either do not circulate or can be checked out for brief periods, are found in the reserve section. You will find on reserve books that teachers feel students should use.

5. Main desk. The main desk is the heart of the library. Here books are checked out and returned. If you cannot find a book on the shelf or encounter other difficulties, the person on duty at the desk will be glad to help or refer you to someone who can help you.

A cautionary note should be added about library use. Like the supermarket, a library operates on a self-service principle. Library staff members are more than willing to offer assistance if you have problems, but you are expected to proceed as far as you can on your own. In other words, don't walk up to the main desk, announce your topic, and expect a full list of available sources on your topic to appear automatically. Librarians will expect you to know the basic tools in the library and how to use them. Do not hesitate to ask for assistance if you need it, but don't expect the librarian to do your work for you.

A. *Using the card catalogue*
The card catalogue is a list of all the books in the library.

It is, therefore, the starting point for building a bibliography. Each book is listed on at least three cards—author's card, title card, and the subject card—all in one alphabetical list. Why is a book catalogued on three different cards? To be helpful to you, the user.

If you look for the title alphabetically in the catalogue, you will find it. The same is true concerning the author. In this instance, you would seek the author's name in its proper alphabetical place and find the card listing the title and subject area.

Most likely, however, you will go to the card catalogue without titles or authors in mind, but with a topic idea and at least a notion of the subject. Let's return to our Gettysburg example. You may find one book whose exact title is *The Battle of Gettysburg.* Then what? You know this subject comes under the heading of history, American history, the American Civil War. You now have several other categories in which to look. Significant names involved in that conflict are also excellent ideas. People like Lee, Meade, Longstreet, and Pickett were engaged in the Gettysburg campaign. Look under their names in the catalogue.

When you go to the stack area to pick up a particular book you want, look around in the section where that book is located. You may find other books you want sitting beside the one you went to pick up.

Libraries cross-refer the cards in the catalogue. Laced throughout the catalogue will be cards with "See" or "See also" at the top. Such cards will list other headings under which you will find additional sources on your topic. *Be on the lookout for these cards.* Jot down the subject heading on a piece of paper so you can look under these headings later. Most research difficulties encountered by students occur because they do not seek out cross-references. They are indispensable for building a good bibliography.

B. *Guidelines to card catalogue information*
A library may have millions of volumes. Even in a modest library, no one person can possibly know all the books and periodicals (magazines). Therefore, it is important to have a system of classification that is clear both to the library staff and the users. The card catalogue, with its numbering system, is that system of classification:

The following hints will help you as you work in the catalogue.

1. A man's works are listed first; works about him follow.

2. Abbreviations and numbers are alphabetized as if they were written in full. *Dr. Faustus,* for example, would be catalogued as if it were *Doctor Faustus.* Names which begin with *Mc* or *M'* are filed under *Mac.* In the catalogue, *101 Easy Recipes* would be filed *One Hundred and One Easy Recipes.*

3. Prefixes like *von* and articles—*a, an,* and *the* (and articles in foreign languages) are omitted from the alphabetical filing. *The Roman Way* by Edith Hamilton would be filed under *Roman Way.*

4. Subdivisions of a subject are listed alphabetically. An exception is history. Here subdivisions are filed chronologically.

5. The basic form of the catalogue card is the author's card. The title and subject cards are the same except the title or subject heading is written above the author's name and filed alphabetically according to title or subject. Sometimes the subject headings are typed in

red or in capital letters to distinguish them from author and title cards.

C. *Information on the catalogue card*

The information contained on a card follows a standard form if the library uses a printed card supplier. This information is thorough yet brief. It will include:

1. Call number (classification number). This number is needed to find the book in the stacks.

2. Author of the book.

3. Title of the book.

4. Publisher, place of publication, and year published.

5. Book's size, number of pages, illustrations, and plates.

6. Other information useful to the user. For example, if a book has a bibliography, it is specified. Often it will tell the length of the bibliography. A bibliography at the end of a book is an excellent way to build your working bibliography.

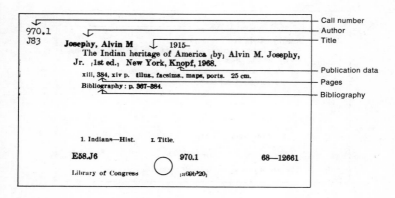

A title card:

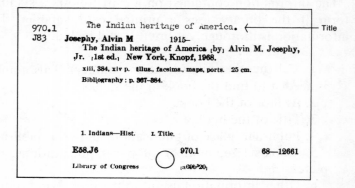

A subject card:

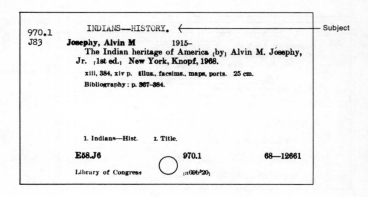

D. *Finding books in a library*

Every book in a library has its own call number and its place on a shelf. Not only will the card catalogue tell you if the library has a particular book, but the card will also tell you where you will find the book. The call number (or classification number) is the key to a book's location. Books are divided into categories according to subject matter and then placed on the shelves according to these groupings. That's why you can go to the shelf looking for a particular book and find other books on your topic next to the book you are looking for.

The most common system used is the Dewey Decimal Classification System. This system was devised in the last century and has now gained wide acceptance in libraries. According to this plan, books are divided into ten groups and assigned numbers. Some libraries don't classify fiction books but place them on the shelves alphabetically according to the author's last name.

The ten groups in the Dewey System are:

000-099 Generalities (*e.g.* bibliographies and catalogues, general encyclopedic works, general periodicals, newspapers, and journalism).

100-199 Philosophy and related disciplines (*e.g.*, psychology is grouped in this category).

200-299 Religion.

300-399 The social sciences (*e.g.* political science, economics, law, and education).

400-499 Language (subdivided by the language families, *e.g.* English and Anglo-Saxon, under which you will find dictionaries, etymologies, grammars, etc.).

500-599 Pure science (*e.g.* mathematics, astronomy

and allied sciences, physics, chemistry and allied sciences).

600-699 Technology—applied sciences (*e.g.* medical sciences, engineering and allied operations, business and related enterprises, and buildings).

700-799 The arts (*e.g.* arthitecture, painting and paintings, photography and photographs, and music).

800-899 Literature and rhetoric (like 400-499, this category is subdivided first into the language families, with subtopics such as drama, poetry, fiction, and letters under each language).

900-999 General geography, history, and related disciplines.

E. *Sources for your bibliography in the reference section*
One of the best places to begin your bibliographic search is the reference section in the library. This is particularly true if your general knowledge of your chosen topic is limited. Articles found in encyclopedias, magazines, and newspapers will often include suggested readings and perhaps specific references to authoritative books that relate to the subject.

Libraries will contain some or all of the following reference sources:

ATLASES
Atlases, in addition to their extremely useful maps, include information about climate, geographical features, prominent cities, and brief sketches of historic, economic, and social developments. Be sure to choose the latest edition possible because the names and boundaries of countries are constantly changing.

Good atlases are invaluable for background information.

The International Atlas. Rand McNally. A basic work.
Rand McNally New Cosmopolitan World Atlas.
Strong emphasis on the United States and outlying
possessions. Includes colored maps for the individual states, with inserts for large cities.

Shepherd, William R. *Historical Atlas.* Covers the
period 1450 B.C. to current times. Expecially good
for colored maps showing battle strategies, growth
of commerce, and what treaties did to boundaries.

Webster's Geographical Dictionary. Gives the usual
gazeteer information of location, area, population,
altitudes of mountains, etc., for 40,000 place
names. Also contains historical names from biblical
times, ancient Greece and Rome, medieval Europe,
and the two World Wars. Includes black and white
maps of the individual states of the United States,
as well as foreign countries. This is an excellent
source for quickly finding the names of all the
provinces of France, for discovering that Germany
has two Frankfurts, and for knowing that Hampton
Roads is a "channel . . . through which the James,
Elizabeth, and Nansemond Rivers flow into Chesa-
peake Bay."

BIOGRAPHY

An excellent source of information, often overlooked by
students, is the biographical dictionary. These dictionaries
may be useful to you in research.

Biographical Index. A finding source, published four
times a year, which indexes books in English and
some 1500 periodicals. For example, the February
1970 volume lists two magazine articles on Mick
Jagger and two books and one article on Bertrand

Russell. It has an "Index to Professions and Occupations," which lists people under the various topics (*e.g.* Mayors—American, Civil Rights Leaders, Spies).

Current Biography. Published monthly, with annual volumes. Informal, readable sketches of personalities prominent in the media. The 1968 volume opens with essays on Ralph David Abernathy, General Creighton Abrams, Gardiner Ackley, Spiro Agnew, Alvin Ailey, Saul Alinsky, Svetlana Alliluyeva. Each yearly volume has an index to the previous years in the decade. The index in the 1968 volume reveals that the jazz composer, Miles Davis, was a subject in the volume for June 1962.

Dictionary of American Biography. The authoritative source for Americans no longer living. Contains over 13,000 subjects in signed articles, accompanied by bibliographies.

Slocum, Robert B. *Biographical Dictionaries and Related Works.* A bibliographical tool listing biographical sources, mainly according to geography and vocation. For example, four biographical dictionaries are listed under the subject, "Southern States," with additional dictionaries and source books listed under the individual Southern states.

Webster's Biographical Dictionary. A quick reference source for basic information on over 40,000 people from ancient times to the present.

Who's Who. A yearly dictionary of prominent living people, with the main emphasis on those in Great Britain.

Who's Who in America. Published every other year. This is a dictionary of prominent living Americans, giving brief biographical data and addresses.

ENCYCLOPEDIAS

Encyclopedias are the first place to look for information in the reference section. Check through all the encyclopedias in the library. Also examine the encyclopedia index (usually the last volume) for cross-references to your topic. Several, like the *Americana* and *Britannica*, have a bibliography following each major article. Books listed following an article are the standard works on the subject and are indispensable for your bibliography.

The following may be useful to you:

Collier's Encyclopedia. This is a general encyclopedia which has a readable style. It is strong on science, technology, philosophy, classics, and biography. The last volume contains a detailed index and a classified bibliography of some 12,000 titles which include films and other materials as well as books. By being in a separate volume, the bibliographies can be updated more frequently than the basic set. Supplemented by *Collier's Encyclopedia Year Book.*

Columbia Encyclopedia. This is a one-volume encyclopedia, useful for identification and brief articles.

Encyclopedia Americana. A good, popular encyclopedia. It is sometimes preferred by students because it is easier to read than the *Britannica*. It is especially strong on American places, organizations, and institutions. There is excellent material on countries, literature, poetry, industry, science, technology, and biography, with valuable book, drama, and opera digests. *The American Annual*, published each year, accompanies the set.

Encyclopaedia Britannica. This is the most scholarly encyclopedia, and it is respected in academic work. The articles are long and are written by authorities in the respective fields. Note that the maps are located in the very useful index volume. The basic set is supplemented by the yearbook, *Britannica Book of the Year*, which helps to keep the encyclopedia up to date by covering the events of the preceding year.

HANDBOOKS

Handbooks of various types are on the reference shelves. They assist you in finding the exact wording of a famous phrase and who said it.

> Bartlett, John. *Familiar Quotations.* Famous sayings or writings of English and American authors, with special sections for anonymous, biblical, and other quotations. Arranged chronologically by author.
> Mencken, Henry L. *The American Language.* An invaluable study of words used in America, including slang.
> Stevenson, Burton E. *Home Book of Quotations.* Contains 50,000 extracts from authors of all ages and countries. Arrangement is by subject, with index.
> Wentworth, Harold and S. B. Flexner. *Dictionary of American Slang.*

ALMANACS AND YEARBOOKS

Almanacs not only predict the weather, but also have valuable information—statistics, facts, and world records of every kind. These almanacs and yearbooks may be in your library.

> *Facts on File.* Digests of the significant news of the

day from a number of metropolitan dailies. The facts are recorded day by day.

New York Times Almanac.

Statesman's Yearbook. Data about the governments of the world, such as constitution and form of government, economic conditions, religion, defenses, and diplomatic representatives. Good bibliography of statistical and reference sources for each country.

U.S. Bureau of the Census. *Statistical Abstract of the United States.* Annual digest of data collected by statistical agencies of the U. S. Covers population, vital statistics, finance, cost of living, etc.

World Almanac.

Reader's Guide to Periodical Literature

The best sources of information on current topics are magazine articles. You will find an index of these articles from over 100 publications in the *Reader's Guide to Periodical Literature. Reader's Guide* is published twice a month. Every quarter, the previous two month's entries are put together with the current month and published in one alphabetical listing. At the end of the year, the annual edition is published. Libraries keep all volumes—bi-weeklies, quarterlies, and the annual volumes.

Therefore, you have an index of magazines as recent as two weeks ago. And the index extends back in the past as far as you care to trace your topic.

Reader's Guide is arranged much like the card catalogue. Articles are listed under the author's name and under at least one subject heading.

To conserve space, this guide has its own abbreviation system. A sample page from *Reader's Guide* follows.

Reader's Guide Facsimile and Explanatory Notes

AFRICA
Native races
Threat of African tribalism. M. C. Hubbard.
[il] Atlan 207:45-7 Ja '61 —————————————— Illustrated
Politics
White and black in Africa. P. Duignan and
L. H. Gann. il Nat R 10:47-9 Ja 28 '61

AIKMAN, Lonnelle
Inside the White House. Nat Geog Mag [119:]
1-43 Ja '61 —————————————————————— Volume number

AIRLINES
Consolidations and mergers
Trunks oppose United-Capital merger. Avia-
tion W 74:41 [Ja 30 '61] —————————————— January 30, 1961
Fares
Hawaiian, Aloha airlines urging common
fares from the mainland. Aviation W 74:43
F 6 '61
United States
[See also] names of airlines, e.g. United
air lines ——————————————————————————— Cross-reference

AIRPLANE engines
Noise
See Airplanes—Noise

AIRPLANES
Electra on public trial. L. Davis. il Flying
68 [46-7]+ F '61 ———————————————————— Pages 46-47
Noise
Thrust lever. D. Kuhn. Flying 68:92 F '61

AIRPLANES in patrol work
[Flying fish and game warden.] F. A. Tinker.
il Flying 68:44-5+ F '61 ——————————————— Title of article

ALBEE, Edward
American dream. Criticism
[New Yorker] 36:62+ F 4 '61 ————————————— Magazine
Time il por 77:53+ F 3 '61

ALCESTIS; opera. See Gluck, C. W.

ALGERIA
Politics and government
Algeria and the French left. T. Molnar.
Nat R 10:51 Ja 28 '61
Toward peace in Algeria. New Repub 144:7-8
F 6 '61

AMERICAN dream; drama. See Albee, E.

AQUARIUMS
Open secret: the wonderful world of little
fishes. [bibliog] il McCalls 88:50-7 Ja '61 ———— Bibliography

KEY TO ABBREVIATIONS

Study the explanatory notes carefully in order to under-
stand the abbreviation system.

Some libraries use the *Abridged Reader's Guide*. It is
basically the same as *Reader's Guide* except the abridged
version does not list as many periodicals.

OTHER PERIODICAL INDEXES

Applied Science and Technology Index. Monthly,
with quarterly and annual cumulations. Subject
index to about 200 engineering and technical periodicals in aeronautics, automation, chemistry, con-
struction, metallurgy, transportation, etc.

Public Affairs Information Service. *Bulletin.* Weekly.
A subject index to periodicals, books, pamphlets,
documents (including the publications of the U.S.
Government), society publications, and mimeo-
graphed material relating to economic and social
conditions, public administration, etc.

International Index. Quarterly, with annual and larger
cumulations. This is an index to periodicals in the
social sciences and humanities, with three-fourths of
them being published in the United States. In 1965,
its name was changed to:

Social Sciences & Humanities Index.

OTHER SOURCES OF INFORMATION

You can find additional titles by using reference books
which lead to further sources. The best beginning books
are the bibliographies of bibliographies, that is, those
reference tools which list bibliographies on specific subjects.

Library of Congress Catalog—Books: Subjects

Some libraries have this Library of Congress index on the reference shelf. If you can find a library that has it, you are very fortunate. It is published three times a year. Then, these quarterly issues are gathered into one volume covering the entire year. Finally, every five years, the yearly volumes are collected into one set.

The Library of Congress Subject Index is a tool limited to "books, phamphlets, maps, atlases, periodicals, and other serials" which are in the Library of Congress. But the materials in this index are generally available at other research libraries. (Research libraries would include large public libraries, state libraries, and college and university libraries. Your librarian can help you obtain materials from such libraries through the "library loan" system. You may want to discuss this possibility with him. It must be emphasized, however, that it takes time to receive materials from other libraries through the loan system. Plan your work schedule for the paper carefully.)

The volumes in the Library of Congress Subject Index contain reductions of Library of Congress catalogue cards arranged according to subject. Under the subject of your research, you will find titles of books on that particular subject. Also, you will often find the subtopic, "Bibliography," following the specific topic.

The general usefulness of the index is illustrated by the subject "Abraham Lincoln" (arranged under Lincoln, Abraham). The January-March 1970 volume lists two works on Lincoln himself, followed by one or more books on such subtopics as "Anecdotes," "Military Leadership," and "Views on Slavery." Other subtopics on Lincoln are covered in other volumes. The 1968 volume lists 14 books on Lincoln and also on the subtopics, "Assassination," "Journey to New England, Feb.-Mar., 1860," "Journey to Washington, February, 1861," and "Political Career before 1861." Of special interest to research is the 1960-64 volume. Under Lincoln, four books are listed under the subtopic, "Bibliography."

This index is the quickest, most complete, and most up-to-date source of books available for your bibliography. The only limiting factor is your writing speed.

Bibliographic Index

This index is published quarterly, with annual and larger collections. It lists bibliographies which are in books and in magazines. The index covers a large group of specific topics and has excellent cross-references.

For example, the 1963-65 volume has six books and one magazine that contain bibliographies about Abraham Lincoln. It also has a subtopic, "Portraits," under which there is an intriguing title, *Lincoln in Photographs: An Album of Every Known Pose.*

The Reader's Adviser

This is an annotated guide, arranged by subject, to actual books on particular subjects. It is more than a reference book that only lists titles. The book is published frequently to take advantage of the latest titles.

In the 11th edition, the "Modern American Fiction" chapter contains a short introductory essay and subchapters, "Historical Studies and Critical Works," "Recent Collections of Modern Short Stories," and "Fiction by Black Americans."

Under individual authors, you will find their works currently in print, a paragraph or two discussing the author (often spliced with quotations from reviews), and concluding with a list of books on the author.

For example, LeRoi Jones' works are found under both "Modern American Poetry" and "American Drama."

Newspaper Index

Libraries generally keep at least one prominent newspaper on file for research. Some libraries keep the *New York Times* and have the *New York Times Index* on the reference shelf. This index will help you locate articles on any subject covered in the *Times*. The *Times Index* is very useful in locating material in other newspapers because it gives a clue to the date of events.

In most instances the newspapers are kept on microfilm to preserve space and prevent deterioration of the paper. The best thing for you to do is check with the librarian. Find out what newspaper the library has bound or on microfilm, and use that paper.

While you are doing your research, you have probably noticed that the best books are the ones closest to the source. For example, the best book for a paper on the Beatles would be a book written by a Beatle. If you can't find that, an interview published by a magazine or newspaper would be excellent.

If you are writing on a local subject, like air pollution in County X, you might find a knowledgeable person to interview yourself. Be sure to quote him exactly even if you have to write during the interview.

On up-to-date topics, like reactions to latest Supreme Court decisions or local political issues, you will probably be forced to use interviews to gather material.

In any of the above examples, you will be gathering material from what is called "primary" sources. Primary sources are the best for any research paper because they produce new ideas. Your conclusions and judgments based on primary sources may be so original that they present your teacher with ideas he hasn't thought about.

If you are writing on a historical topic, don't assume that primary sources are out of the question. Most prominent historical figures wrote a great deal of material that you can find in the library. You won't be able to read the complete works of Thomas Jefferson for a paper. You will find Jefferson material valuable for your paper mentioned in books *about* Jefferson (secondary sources). To quote Jefferson directly will give your paper more weight than if you quote someone else quoting Jefferson.

You may list your primary sources separately at the beginning of your bibliography. The list should include diaries, autobiographies, letters, interviews, speeches, documents, and books by the person who is the subject of the paper. A list of primary sources would strengthen your paper.

Compiling a working bibliography

A research paper will require a bibliography at the end of the paper. This bibliography (as opposed to a working bibliography) is a list of all sources used in writing the paper. A working bibliography, however, is a list of all possible sources available for your paper. When you begin to read, you will discover that some sources in your working bibliography have no value for the paper. These sources would not be included in your final bibliography.

In preparing for your research, you should keep two separate files of note cards: (1) for bibliography and (2) for your notes. Using cards is the best system because cards can be easily rearranged and located when you start to write. Do not use a notebook.

Most students have discovered that 3 x 5 or 4 x 6 file cards are suitable for bibliography and notes. Buy at least several packs.

A typical bibliographic card for a book would look like this:

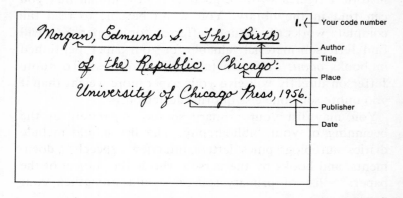

For bibliography, use only one side of the card for each book or other source. A bibliographic card will require this information:

1. Author(s) of book or article (also editor, edition, or translator where applicable).

2. Title of book (as found on title page), or article and magazine.

3. Publication information—place, publisher, date (and volume number if applicable).

4. Your own code number. Assigning every source its own code number is the most important time-saving practice in your note-taking system.

When you make out a bibliographic card, give it a code number and put the number in the upper right-hand corner of the card. Later, when you are taking notes from a book, give the note card the same code number as your bibliographic card for that particular book.

You will save hours of time if you cross-refer your bibliographic and note cards in this manner.

For a magazine:

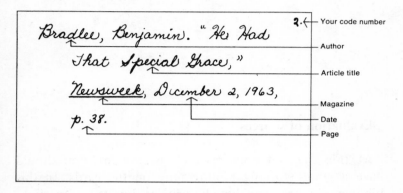

Note that the form of the information on the card is exactly as it should appear in your bibliography at the end of the paper. We suggest that you set up your cards correctly because it will save hours of time when you complete your final bibliography.

In the chapter, "Bibliography and Footnote Samples," you will find a list of the source variations you may encounter in documentation. Check this list for correct form if you are in doubt about a particular source and its bibliographic card.

Be sure to make out the bibliographic cards thoroughly and accurately. When writing a final bibliography, many students have despaired because they discovered they hadn't taken down all the information they needed. If the library is closed and the paper is due the next morning, this situation is serious.

CHAPTER IV

Researching the paper

Evaluation of sources

At this stage of your research assignment, you should have a good working bibliography on file cards. In this bibliography are encyclopedia articles, books, and periodicals that relate (in some degree) to your topic. The teacher may require you to turn in this bibliography as a check on your progress.

The question is, however, "How do I know which source or sources will be the best for my topic? I have so much material, and I don't have time to read it all. How do I pick and choose?"

Good judgment in source selection plays an important part in a good research paper. Such judgment is not left to chance but follows common sense and rules which you should apply. Here are suggestions to evaluate a source:

1. Author. On the jacket or at the end of the preface, you may find the professional qualifications of the author. From these "credits," you can judge the author's authoritativeness.

2. Title. In some instances, careful selection of sources according to the complete title is helpful in choosing potential sources for your topic.

3. Date of publication. For a current or technological topic, the publication date on the title page or the back of the title page can determine a book's relative usefulness. Look for the copyright date on the back of the title page. It is designated by a small "c" in a circle followed by a date. This is a clue to the date of the material itself. Sometimes, the title page will have 1969, but the copyright date will be 1942. This means the particular edition was published in 1969. However, the book was written and first published in 1942.

4. Foreword or preface. Students have a tendency to skip the foreword of the book. Authors often state the purpose and guiding theme of their book in the preface. It can be very helpful.

5. Table of contents. The table of contents gives you the chapters and direction of a book. You may quickly find the useful section by checking this table.

6. Index. The index is even more specific than the table of contents in locating information you might need for the paper.

Types of material

All forms of research material fall into two main categories: factual and interpretative. You should be able to make a distinction between the two. Students often are misled because they assume that an interpretation is a fact. For example, Richard M. Nixon won the presidential election in 1968. That is a fact. The reasons for his victory are interpretations.

You should distinguish between types of material in your reading and also in your own writing.

Reading

The most time-consuming part of a research paper is the reading involved. If you allow yourself plenty of time, it is a pleasurable adventure. If you're trying to meet a deadline for your paper, it may be a frantic experience.

Your research reading will have two different purposes. The first is skimming, and it helps you make a quick judgment about the value of a source. It also helps you locate the pertinent sections in a book that relate to your topic. The way you skim will vary according to your reading style and the author's writing style. Below are general guidelines to follow, however:

1. Read the foreword and table of contents.
2. Note the chapter titles and subheadings. These often contain hints for possible units in your outline and are helpful in determining the value of a particular chapter or subdivision.
3. Read the first and last paragraphs of each chapter.
4. Read the first and last sentences of each paragraph. This is particularly important if you decide the chapter has valuable information for your research.
5. Don't take notes when you are skimming. After skimming and deciding a chapter or subheading is important, then read the entire unit carefully and take notes.

Taking notes

Taking notes for a research paper differs from the system you use for the classroom. For research, the best system is the note card. We suggested earlier that you use cards for your bibliographic file. The same type of card is ideal for the notes.

Each piece of information should be written on a separate card (one side only). In the upper right-hand corner, write your own code number which identifies the book you are using. Having to supply a code number on the note card will remind you that a bibliographic card should exist for this source.

After you have recorded the information, be sure to add the page or pages on which you found the information. (Title, author, and publication data will be on the bibliographic card.)

Many students find it useful to label the entry on a note card to identify information without reading the complete card. These "slugs," as they are sometimes called, will permit greater speed and accuracy in rearranging the cards for the final outline.

Here is a sample note card set up according to the above procedures:

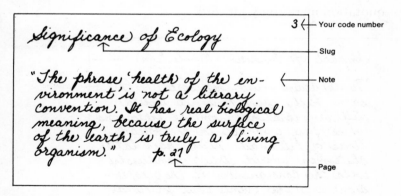

Basically, there are two types of information you will enter on a note card. The first is called a "summary card." Let's suppose an author has extended remarks in a specific section. These comments are valuable for your paper. Rather than quote the section in its entirety, summarize the section and put it on the card in your own words. Most of your note cards will be of this type.

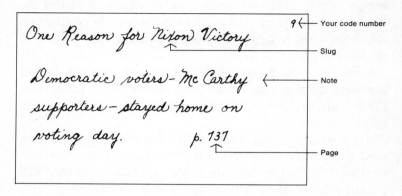

The second form of information you will need is the direct quotation. If you wish to quote a particular author, copy the sentence or paragraph exactly and place it within quotation marks on your card.

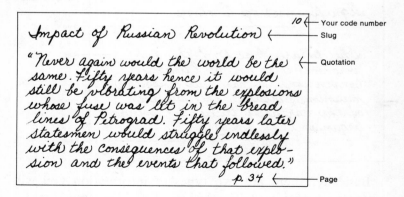

You may wish to use only parts of a sentence. In this

case, use an ellipsis, three spaced periods (. . .) to indicate the omitted material.

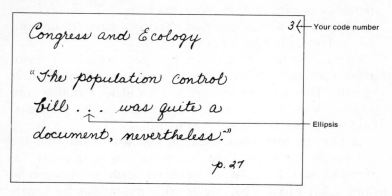

Note the space before the first dot and after the last one. This is the proper form for an ellipsis.

A period and three spaced dots indicate that an omission came (1) at the end of a sentence, (2) the first part of the next sentence, and (3) a whole sentence or more.

The brackets around "Mencken" below are additions by the writer to explain the antecedent of "he." Brackets are used to indicate explanation by a writer in a quotation.

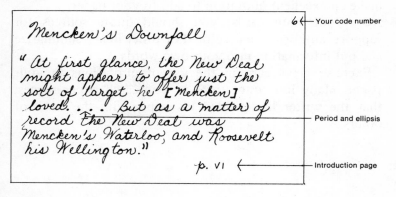

However, the two types of note cards—summary and quotation—pose a question. How can you tell whether to quote or summarize in your own words? There is no simple answer to this question. You will have to use your own judgment but guidelines do exist.

Suppose an author makes what you consider a major point for your paper. In such a case, quote the writer exactly. This will give *support* to your ideas. Building your position with quotations by authorities in the particular field will prove your good judgment.

As you dig into your research, you will notice that the experts do not agree. Their interpretations of an event, for example, will differ. If you disagree with one interpretation, substantiate your views with quotations by others who do agree with you. Quotations from the authorities will cement your position.

Finally, quotations will add color and vividness to your paper. For example, let's say your paper is on the environmental crisis. In your reading, you discover a quotation by Mark Twain. He once described the Mississippi River as being "too thick to drink and too thin to plow." This describes the pollution of American rivers, and it would make an excellent quotation to add to your paper.

On your note cards, you should quote sources for support, authority, and color. For other items, summarize and put information into your own words.

Exercise great care in the use of quotations in your paper. Many long quotations in a research paper suggest that the writer has padded his paper with the work of others.

A check on your note system

After you have completed your first note card, check your system to see if you have all the necessary information to write a footnote from only your material. Do not use the book in this check.

You will need both the bibliographic card and the note card to make a footnote. From your own code number on the note card, you will be able to locate the bibliographic card which has the same number. The bibliographic card will supply you with title, author, and place, publisher, and date of publication. Your note card will give you the specific page of the source for the footnote. These are the basic items of a footnote.

If you do not have the necessary information on cards, something is wrong with your system. Determine what you've left out and make sure you include all information necessary from this point on. You must do it correctly because the book may not be with you when you start to place the footnotes in the final copy of the paper.

CHAPTER V

Final outline, rough draft and revision

Final outline

By the time you are ready to establish a final outline, you have finished your research and taken the notes needed for your paper. You have two aids to help you make the final outline: (1) the preliminary outline, and (2) your note file with appropriate "slug" headings.

The key to an outline is logic. A good outline, and consequently a good paper, builds one block at a time. It should be clear in your final outline why the sections have been chosen and why they fall into a particular order. Remember, a final outline is a framework for another person. He should have no difficulty in following your line of thought in the outline.

There are several useful hints to aid you in determining this framework for the outline.

1. Time sequence. Many papers naturally fall into a chronological outline. Battles, events, and biographies can easily be outlined in this fashion.

2. Pro and con. Building your outline on arguments for and against a particular subject is ideal in some

cases. You can build the blocks of the paper according to the strengths of the various positions. Save the best or strongest (and yours) for last. An outline like this has a natural progression.

In making the final decision about your outline, the following procedures may be helpful. Review your preliminary outline and the "slug" headings on your note cards. Don't write anything down at this point. Just mull over the outline question in your mind for several days, if need be. Then, come back to your desk and write, without reference to anything, what you feel is the best possible outline. After you have finished, compare it with the preliminary outline, looking for the relative strengths and weaknesses of the two outlines. Then combine the two into what you feel is the best possible.

Ask yourself these questions. Is the outline logical? Can I explain why this section of the paper comes before another? Will the reader be able to easily follow this outline? If you can answer *yes* to these questions, you have a good final outline to write your rough draft.

Rearrange your note cards according to the final outline. When the various sections and subdivisions are in the proper sequence, you're almost ready to write. You may discover, however, that a particular section (or sections)

needs further research to flesh it out in equal proportion to the others in the outline and file cards. If this is the case, then it's back to the drawing board—to the library for more research in the weak areas.

Rough draft

In writing the rough draft, the value of clear, accurate note cards becomes apparent. On these cards is a tremendous amount of information, arranged in proper order, to guide you in writing.

Set aside three or four hours to allow yourself sufficient time to write without interruption. If possible, write the entire paper in one sitting. Don't worry about grammar, sentence structure, punctuation, or spelling (if in doubt, circle the word in question). The purpose of a rough draft is to get your ideas on paper, nothing more or less. Revision and cleaning up the rough edges will come later.

Leave wide margins on either side of the page and double or triple space between lines. This will allow you ample room for corrections and additions.

Be sure you copy all quotations correctly. It isn't necessary at this point to write out the footnotes. In the text, jot down the author and page number (Mencken, p. 10) following the quotation for quick reference when you set up the footnotes.

One final point needs to be mentioned. You will discover as you write that some of the note cards are not necessary for your paper. Resist the temptation to use every card in your file. If the note is necessary or useful for the paper, include it. If not, put it aside. Be ruthless in applying a critical eye to your notes. It's better to reject a note card than to cross out an entire section of your rough draft.

Once you have finished the rough draft, the sense of pride and satisfaction will begin to seep through. You're not finished yet, but you're a long way from the beginning. That feeling of accomplishment will give you the lift to push on and do the best job you can.

Revision

After you've finished your rough draft, put it aside. Don't look at it for a while. Wait as long as a week if possible. This break will help you come back to the paper with a fresh and critical eye. You will be able to examine it almost as if it were someone else's work. That's good because you will be a better critic.

Read the paper through completely and quickly. Don't stop to correct or make changes. Just note in the margin the obvious flaws and keep reading. You need an over-all impression before you start making revisions.

Every writer—professional or student—hates to use an editing pencil on his own writing. Ruthless criticism and cutting, however, will probably be necessary if you want to turn in a quality paper.

Begin making your revisions on your second reading. The following guide will help you find the basic flaws that are common in a rough draft.

1. Cut all words, phrases, sentences, and even paragraphs that don't contribute to the theme and purpose of the paper. Do not be afraid to cut and rewrite.

2. Vary the sentence length. Short sentences are not a sign of ignorance.

3. Check the sentence arrangement in paragraphs. A paragraph in which every sentence begins with "The" is

boring. Begin one sentence with a prepositional phrase, another with a clause, and a third with a noun. Variety in arrangement will add immeasurably to your style, but don't overdo it.

4. Examine the verbs. Make them strong and direct. Sentences that begin "There is . . ." and "There are . . ." indicate a lazy writer. Use them with great care.

5. Pay particular attention to the beginning and closing of your paper. Remember, the first paragraph sets the reader's attitude about the entire paper. Does the beginning "grab" the reader's attention? Make it your best.

Will the reader know he has come to the end of the paper only because the next page is the bibliography? It should summarize and conclude the whole paper.

6. Watch the transitions, the changes of topic or ideas in paragraphs and sections. Your reader won't know what you mean, only what you say. Have you given him sufficient "signposts" so he can follow you?

7. Careless errors are the ones that hurt. Check your grammar, punctuation, and spelling.

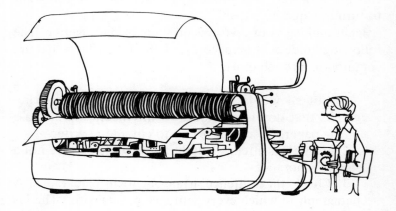

Proofreader's marks will be useful in editing your paper.

Mark	Example	Meaning
¶		Paragraph
no ¶		No paragraph
⌃ ⌃		Insert comma, insert semicolon
∪	carefl**u**l	Transpose
ℐ	the man ~~who~~	Take out
stet	~~quickly~~ read	Leave it in
⌐		Move left
⌐		Move right
lc	Northern part	Lower case (small letter)
uc	indians	Upper case (capital letter)
#	follow⌃the	Insert space
⌒	writ⌣ing	Close up
⊙	trans⊙	Insert period
⋀	man⌃away *ran*	Insert word
○	⟨LC⟩	A circle around abbreviations means spell out

CHAPTER VI

Documentation

Documentation is an expression of credit. You have used other people's ideas and writings in your paper. It is both honest and required that you give credit where credit is due. To use the ideas or to quote another's work without giving credit is actually stealing. This is called plagiarism. Plagiarism is a serious offense and grounds for the rejection of a research paper. Make sure you document *all* the sources you use in your paper.

Documentation in a research paper takes two forms: bibliography and footnotes. Your teacher may have specific requirements for the form of documentation he wants you to use. If so, make sure you have a clear understanding of the form he wants for bibliography and footnotes.

On the other hand, he may leave the matter entirely up to you. The most important point about documentation is consistency. Once you have decided on the form you want to use for bibliography and footnotes, stick to this form throughout the paper. This point is emphasized for one reason. There are a number of forms used in writing footnotes and bibliography, and no one form is "correct." All are acceptable, but not all in the same paper!

We have chosen a widely-used but simple form of

documentation as a guide in this book. It is the form recommended by the Modern Language Association in their *MLA Style Sheet*. The form of documentation in the *Style Sheet* is used by many professional journals, colleges and universities, and teachers.

Bibliography

You have already established a working bibliography to locate possible sources for your paper. It was suggested that you set up items on the bibliographic file card properly. If you have done so, the task of setting up your bibliography will be relatively simple.

Your bibliography should include all the sources you have either read or used (as footnotes) in the paper. Go through your bibliographic card file and pull out these cards. Make sure the cards are in alphabetical order according to the author's last name. If the book has more than one author, the card should be alphabetized according to the first author listed on the title page of the book.

The basic bibliographic forms are:

FOR A BOOK

The items of a bibliographic entry are:

Morgan, Edmund S. The Birth of the Republic. Chicago: University
    of Chicago Press, 1956.

1. Author. Name is inverted (last name first) because a bibliography is alphabetized.
2. Title. Titles of books, magazines, or any published unit are underlined.
3. Place of publication, publisher, and year published.

Note the colon after the place of publication. If the publication has had several printings, use the most recent one.

4. Punctuation. Note that items for a book entry are separated with periods and that entry is closed with a period.

5. Spacing. The second and following lines of an entry are indented five spaces (1/2″). This is called "hanging indentation." Lines in a bibliographic entry are single spaced; entries are double spaced.

FOR A MAGAZINE

Bradlee, Benjamin. "He Had That Special Grace," Newsweek, December 2, 1963, p. 38.

The basic magazine entry differs from the book entry.

1. Author. Form is same as a book.

2. Article title. Comes before the name of magazine and is set off with quotation marks.

3. Magazine title. Underlined as a book.

4. Date of publication. Note that a comma follows the date.

5. Page number. Page or pages are specified with Arabic numbers, preceded with page abbreviation (p.).

6. Punctuation. Author's name is closed with a period and entry ends with period. Other items of magazine entry are separated by commas.

7. Spacing. Form is same as a book entry.

Form for bibliography page in paper

The bibliography page should be numbered as a page of

the paper. The word BIBLIOGRAPHY (all capital letters) should be approximately 3″ below page number and centered on page. Drop another 3″ and begin bibliographic entries flush with left-hand margin. Follow usual margins at right and bottom of page.

Footnotes

A footnote is a credit for a particular quotation or idea used in the paper. Its purpose is to give the reader a specific reference to the location of that source. A footnote may also be an explanation of a point you do not feel is important enough to include in the body of the paper. For example, the first time you might refer to the North Atlantic Treaty Organization. In a footnote, you might tell the reader you will use NATO for later references.

Footnote punctuation - bottom of page

The basic footnote forms are:

FOR A BOOK

[6]Edmund S. Morgan, The Birth of the Republic (Chicago: University of Chicago Press, 1956), p. 111.

The items of the entry are:
1. Superscript. Arabic number set slightly above the line (a superscript). It corresponds to the number on that page in the body of the paper. Note that the superscript has no spacing or punctuation separating it from the author's name.

2. Author. Name is not inverted.

3. Title. Underlined.

4. Place of publication, publisher, and date. Set off in parentheses.

5. Page. Page abbreviation and page in Arabic numbers.

6. Punctuation. Items of footnote are separated by commas.

7. Spacing. Follows normal paragraph indentation. Lines of a footnote are single spaced; footnotes are double spaced.

FOR A MAGAZINE

[7]Benjamin Bradlee, "He Had That Special Grace," Newsweek, December 2, 1963, p. 38.

Students often ask if they can put the footnotes on a separate page at the end of the paper. Such a practice is easier for the writer but more difficult for the reader. In general, do what is easier for the reader—in your case, the teacher who will evaluate your paper. Little things that make his work easier will be to your advantage.

Footnote punctuation - body of paper

To document a source in the text of the paper, place the appropriate Arabic number at the end of the quotation (outside the closing quotation mark) or the source credit. The number is slightly above the line with no punctuation or spacing, like this.[7]

If a quotation in the paper is five lines or more, the procedure is different. Long quotations are single spaced and have single indentation on left margin and single indentation on right margins. Quotation marks are not used.

Here is an example of a long quotation and its treatment in the paper.

> A farmer in Barbour county remembers, "All through the war, people around here had been gettin' these Christmas cards from all kinda places—Denver one year, then the next year it'd be Guam or someplace like that—and openin' them up, they'd read, 'Merry Christmas, George C. Wallace.' I got 'em too, and I couldn't quite figger them out. I thought it was real nice of this young fella, so far away and all and yet bein' so thoughtful, but I wasn't quite sure I knew who this George C. Wallace was, and why he was writin' me. It seemed kinda strange.
>
> Anyway, when the war was over with and the local political races had done got started over the county, I was out in my field one fine spring afternoon plowin', and I happen to look up and see this young fella comin' across the plowed field from the road, like he had just popped up out of nowhere, steppin' real smart and lively across those furrows, already grinnin' and his hand already stretched out, and all of a sudden I knew why I'd been gettin' them nice cards every Christmas . . . ."[1]

[1]Lewis Chester and others, *An American Melodrama: The Presidential Campaign of 1968* (New York: Viking Press, 1969), p. 265, quoting Marshall Frady, *Wallace* (Cleveland: The World Publishing Company, 1968).

You should triple space between the body of the paper and the first footnote on a page. Double space between footnotes, and single space lines of a footnote.

Judging space requirements for footnotes on a page is sometimes difficult, particularly if you are typing the paper. It is a good idea to type out all the footnotes on a page (or two) before you attempt to put them at the bottom of their proper pages. Be sure to double space between the notes and make sure they are written exactly as they will appear on the paper. Writing out the footnotes in this manner will serve as a guide for the amount of space you will need on a particular page of the paper. If you are in doubt about space, leave more than you think you need because a cramped page is less attractive.

Abbreviations used in footnotes.

[15]Ibid.

Ibid., is an abbreviation of the Latin word, *ibidem*, which means "the same place." In footnote usage, it means the same author, the same book, and the same page as the source cited in the footnote *immediately* before it. For example, footnote 15 is taken from the same source as footnote 14.

[18]Ibid., p. 41.

Ibid., in this footnote refers to the same author and same book, but to a different page.

However, there is a word of caution about the use of *Ibid.* You should be familiar with this form and use it in your paper. But, *Ibid.*, used in a succession of footnotes suggests that the writer is too dependent on one research source. Use *Ibid.*, sparingly. Also, remember that *Ibid.*, can only refer to the footnote immediately before it.

[21]Morgan, p. 137.

Once you have given credit for a book in your footnotes, you may make subsequent references to the book in the form cited above. You need just the author's name and the page cited. The reader will know this footnote refers to a book by Edmund S. Morgan cited earlier in the paper.

The following abbreviations are often used in books, particularly in documentation.

Latin abbreviations

cf.	*confer*	compare
e.g.	*exempli gratia*	for example
et.al.	*et alii*	and others (used for more than two)
etc.	*et cetera*	and so forth
i.e.	*id est*	that is
sic		thus or so. (used in quotations to indicate an error in the quotation which you recognize but cannot change because you are quoting. *sic* is set off in brackets [ ]
v.	*vide*	see
vs.	*versus*	against

Other abbreviations

ch.	chs.	chapter(s)
ed.	eds.	editor(s) or edition(s)
fig.	figs.	figure(s)
introd.		introduction
1.	ll.	line(s)
p.	pp.	page(s)

CHAPTER VII

Bibliography and footnote samples

In this chapter, we have listed sample forms of bibliography and footnote. These will be useful as models to help you set up footnotes and bibliographic entries for various research sources. "FN" indicates footnote, and "B," bibliography.

STANDARD FORMS
Book

FN   [1]Edmund S. Morgan, The Birth of the Republic (Chicago: University of Chicago Press, 1956), p. 111.

B   Morgan, Edmund S. The Birth of the Republic. Chicago: University of Chicago Press, 1956.

Magazine

FN   [2]Benjamin Bradlee, "He Had That Special Grace," Newsweek, December 2, 1963, p. 38.

B   Bradlee, Benjamin. "He Had That Special Grace," Newsweek, December 2, 1963, p. 38.

FOR AN ANONYMOUS AUTHOR

FN   [3]"A Whale of a Failure," Time, July 13, 1970, pp. 44-45.

B   "A Whale of a Failure." Time, July 13, 1970, pp. 44-45.

FOR A SPECIFIC EDITION

FN   [4]Clinton Rossiter, The American Presidency, rev. ed. (New York: Harcourt, Brace & World, Inc., 1960), p. 89.

B   Rossiter, Clinton. The American Presidency, rev. ed. New York: Harcourt, Brace & World, Inc., 1960.

FOR AN EDITED BOOK

FN   [5]Garrett De Bell, ed., The Environmental Handbook (New York: Ballantine Books, Inc., 1970), p. 284.

B   De Bell, Garrett, ed. The Environmental Handbook. New York: Ballantine Books, Inc., 1970.

FOR AN ENCYCLOPEDIA

FN   [6]Encyclopedia Americana (1960) vol. 14, p. 640.

B   Encyclopedia Americana (1960), vol. 14, p. 640.

FOR AN INTERVIEW

FN   [7]L. Francis Griffin, Personal Interview, Farmville, Virginia, March 30, 1970.

B   Griffin, L. Francis. Personal Interview on Prince Edward County, Virginia. Farmville, Virginia, March 30, 1970.

FOR AN INTRODUCTION TO A BOOK

FN   [8]Alistair Cooke, "Introduction to H. L. Mencken," The Vintage Mencken (New York: Random House, 1955), p. vi.

B   Cooke, Alistair. "Introduction to H. L. Mencken," The Vintage Mencken, p. vi. New York: Random House, 1955.

FOR CO-AUTHORS

FN   [9]Nancy C. Millet and Helen J. Throckmorton, How to Read
a Short Story (Boston: Ginn and Company, 1969), p. 35.

B   Millet, Nancy C. and Helen J. Throckmorton. How to Read a
Short Story. Boston: Ginn and Company, 1969.

FOR A LETTER

FN   [10]Thomas Wolfe, Personal letter, August 16, 1933.

B   Wolfe, Thomas. Personal letter. August 16, 1933.

FOR MORE THAN TWO AUTHORS

FN   [11]Lewis Chester and others, An American Melodrama: The
Presidential Campaign of 1968 (New York: Viking Press, 1969),
p. 265.

B   Chester, Lewis and others. An American Melodrama: The Presidential
Campaign of 1968. New York: Viking Press, 1969.

FOR A NEWSPAPER

FN   [12]Godfrey Sperling, Jr., "Campus Warning for Nixon," The
Christian Science Monitor, July 1, 1970, p. 1.

B   Sperling, Godfrey, Jr. "Campus Warning for Nixon," The Christian
Science Monitor, July 1, 1970, p. 1.

FOR A PUBLIC DOCUMENT

FN   [13]U.S. Bureau of the Census, Pocket Data Book: USA 1969
(Washington: U.S. Government Printing Office, 1969), p. 36.

B   U.S. Bureau of the Census. Pocket Data Book: USA 1969.
Washington: U.S. Government Printing Office, 1969.

FOR A SELECTION FROM AN ANTHOLOGY

FN   [14]George Orwell, "Politics and the English Language," A Collection of Essays (Garden City: Doubleday & Company, Inc., 1954), p. 162.

B   Orwell, George. "Politics and the English Language," in A Collection of Essays. Garden City: Doubleday & Company, Inc., 1954.

FOR A SERIES

FN   [15]Steven Crane, "The Black Riders," in The Last Part of the 19th Century, ed. Carl Bode and others, American Literature Series (New York: Washington Square Press, Inc., 1966), p. 599.

B   Crane, Steven. "The Black Riders," The Last Part of the 19th Century, ed. Carl Bode and others. American Literature Series. New York: Washington Square Press, Inc., 1966.

FOR A SUBTITLE

FN   [16]Louis Fischer, Gandhi: His Life and Message for the World (New York: The New American Library, 1954), p. 25.

B   Fischer, Louis. Gandhi: His Life and Message for the World. New York: The New American Library, 1954.

FOR A TRANSLATION

FN   [17]Virgil, The Aeneid, trans. John Dryden (New York: Airmont Publishing Company, Inc., 1968), p. 89.

B   Virgil. The Aeneid, trans. John Dryden. New York: Airmont Publishing Company, Inc., 1968.

FOR VOLUMES

FN   [18]Carl Sandburg, Abraham Lincoln (New York: Harcourt, Brace & World, Inc., 1939), vol. 1, p. 131.

B   Sandburg, Carl. Abraham Lincoln. 3 vols. New York: Harcourt, Brace & World, Inc., 1939.

CHAPTER VIII

Final copy preparation

A research paper has three parts: front matter, including title page and contents page; text or body of paper; and bibliography. The order is as follows:

1. Title page (title page of sample paper will serve as model)
2. Table of contents (contents page of sample paper will serve as model)
3. Body of paper
4. Bibliography

Typing your paper or having it typed is strongly recommended. This will make your paper more attractive and easier for your teacher to read. If you are going to write the paper by hand, make it as neat and legible as possible.

Typing hints

1. Use a quality grade bond paper. To make corrections, use erasure tape.

2. Text of the paper should be double spaced.

3. Indent five spaces (1/2") for the first line of a paragraph; second and following lines of paragraph are flush with the left-hand margin.

4. Leave a margin of 1 and 1/2" on all four sides of page.

5. Center main headings on the page; begin text a third of the way down on the page.

6. Subdivisions can be either centered or placed flush with the left-hand margin. If centered, then the main headings should be all capitals or underlined.

7. Leave a space after comma or semicolon.

8. Leave two spaces after end mark punctuation — period, question mark, or exclamation point.

9. Leave two spaces after colon.

10. Triple space between text and first footnote on page.

11. Double space between footnotes.

12. Single space lines in a footnote.

13. Double space between bibliographic entries; single space lines in a bibliographic entry.

14. Number every page on upper right-hand corner, except title page and main heading pages. Do not type page number on chapter heading pages, but include these pages in your numbering sequence.

Once your final copy has been prepared, proofread a final time. Look for typographical errors and omitted punctuation. If it is all right with your teacher, have someone else read your paper. He may notice flaws that you have overlooked. Make sure the footnote and bibliography forms are correct. Does every footnote number in text have a footnote at the bottom of the page?

You're finished. We said at the beginning that you would find great satisfaction in writing this paper. You have created something that is entirely yours. You should feel proud of yourself. Congratulations and good luck on the paper's evaluation.

What Made the Beatles?

by

A. Student

English 205b

October 15, 1977

CONTENTS

Introduction

Chapter heading page should start third of way down.

Never before in the history of pop music has any group
had the impact that the Beatles has had. Frederick Lewis
reported in the New York Times, "Beatlemania . . .
affects all social classes and all levels of intelligence."[1]
The group has broken every record in show business
including those set by Elvis Presley. The Beatles are the
first recording artists to have a record become a million-
seller before its release.

They have been paid the highest salaries ever recorded
in show business. Every national magazine has, at one
time or another, covered some aspect of the Beatle story.
Exactly how Beatlemania started no one is sure. Perhaps,
if it hadn't been for the shrewd management and guidance
of Brian Epstein, the Beatles would have been lost in the
tide of the hundreds of rock groups in England at that
time. But, they weren't. And whether the major
contributing factor to their success was due to Brian
Epstein or the creative talents of the Beatles themselves,
is the point in question.

The purpose of the paper needs emphasis. Set it off as paragraph

---

[1]Capitol Records Biography, March 1968.

See chapter note on p. 1.

Background of the Beatles

In 1956, about the same time American teenagers were

listening to Elvis Presley's "Heartbreak Hotel," 15 year-

old John Lennon was busy forming a rock band in

England called the Quarrymen.

John Winston Lennon was born on October 9, 1940, in

Liverpool, England. Fred and Julia Lennon separated

shortly after their son's birth, ~~leaving~~ John's Aunt Mimi

~~with the major portion of his upbringing.~~[2] *raised him*

John's unsuccessful career began at Dovedale Primary.

In 1952, he was enrolled at Quarry Bank High for Boys

w~~e~~re he landed at the bottom of his class by the end of

the fourth year. John, a typical Liverpudlian roughneck,

fought his way through school. "I was agressive because I

wanted to be popular. I wanted to be the leader. . . . I

wanted everyone to do what I told them to, to laugh at

my jokes and let me be the boss."[3]

A good quotation!

[2]Hunter Davies, The Beatles: The Authorized Biography (New York: Dell Publishing Company, Inc., 1968), p. 7.

[3]Ibid., pp. 14-15.

When John was 15, his mother bought him a guitar and taught him a few banjo chords. He took a handful of guitar lessons, but hadn't achieved much proficiency when he put together a five-piece band—all school chums—and dubbed the group the Quarrymen, appropriately.

On June 15, 1956, John Lennon and his Quarrymen performed at the Woolton village fete in Liverpool. "That was the day," says John, "the day that I met Paul, that it started moving."[4]

John Paul McCartney was born on June 18, 1942, in Liverpool. He entered the Liverpool Institute after he completed his primary school training. Unlike John, Paul excelled in his studies.[5]

Paul was given his first guitar when he was 14. He had followed pop music for about two years, but it wasn't until the emergence of Elvis Presley that he became actively interested.[6]

Not long after their meeting at the village fete, John Lennon asked Paul to join the Quarrymen. His request

[4]Ibid., p. 23.

[5]Peter Hildreth, Name-Dropper (London: McWhirter Publishing Company Ltd., 1970), p. 27.

[6]Davies, p. 33.

Use passive sparingly

was readily accepted. John and Paul spent hours each day

practicing new chords. John was learning the guitar

chords from Paul, *because* as he realized banjo chords would no

longer do. Paul was interested, even at this time, in build-

ing tunes around the new chords that he was learning.

"Since he'd started playing the guitar, he had *t*ried to

make up a few of his own little tunes. . . . Not to be

outdone, John immediately started making up his own

tunes."[7]

Paul introduced George Harrison to John in 1956.

George was interested in joining the Quarrymen, but John

was apprehensive of George because he *George* was so young.

Finally, in 1958, he consented to let him join the g*r*oup.

George Harrison was born in the Wavertree section of

Liverpool on February 25, 1943.[8] Although he and John

had both attended the Dovedale Primary School, they

hadn't met until George introduced them.

George was about 14 when he first strummed a guitar.

He and Paul, who were classmates at the Liverpool

Institute, learned to play their guitars together with the

help of a guitar manual.

Triple space

[7]Ibid., p. 36.

[8]Hildreth, p. 27.

Formation of the Beatles

John, Paul, and George were the only members of the
Quarrymen ~~that~~ who seemed to click consistantly and remain

together. There were other members who were constantly

changing, either as the result of boredom or of John's

sharp tongue.

The Quarrymen became Johnny and the Moondogs

in 1958. The following year, John persuaded a school

chum, Stu Sutcliffe, to buy a bass guitar with the money he

had won in an art show. Stu had never played the guitar.

That didn't matter to John. No one/else had the money to

buy an electric bass. So Stu was invited into the group.

In 1960, prior to being granted an audition with Larry

Parnes, a top rock and roll promoter, the boys decided

to change their name again. They had all been fans of

Buddy Holly and the Crickets, an American pop group.

john especially liked the name, Crickets. As he repeated

the word aloud, he said, "The idea of beetles came into

my head. I decided to spell it BEAtles to make it look like

beat music, just as a joke."[9]

[handwritten margin note:] awkward

In 1960, the boys decided to change their name again before an audition with Larry Parnes, a top rock and roll promoter.

Good quotation

9Davies, pp. 67-71.

Soon after, four nervous young men turned up at the Parnes audition without an established name and without a drummer. They gave their name as the Silver Beatles (a friend suggested the Silver) and auditioned for Parnes with a stand-in drummer. Nevertheless, they were chosen to play a two-week tour of Scotland as the back-up band for a pop singer.

After the Scotland tour, the Beatles returned to England. They were still being offered engagements in rough Teddy-boy places in Liverpool. The group made plans to go to Germany and in the interim, they returned to the Casbah, a club in Liverpool, where they had played as the Quarrymen. The owner of the Casbah had a son, Pete, who played the drums. Paul auditioned him for the Silver Beatles, hired him, and the five boys set off for Hamburg.

It was in 1960 that John, Paul, George, Stu, and Pete arrived in Hamburg. They called themselves the Beatles now. It was Pete's suggestion to drop the Silver from their name.

The Beatles' first engagement in Hamburg was at the raucous and roudy Indra Club. The facilities provided for the boys at the club were inferior and uncomfortable. Their dressing room was a part of the public rest room, and they had to sleep in the basement. Despite the poor conditions, the boys made the best of it and livened up the show at the Indra. They put excitement into their act. They played loudly, sang loudly, and jumped up and down on the stage. John Lennon recalls, "We'd been meek and mild musicans at first, now we became a powerhouse."[10]

While in Germany, the Beatles also made their first recording. It was an album entitled "The Beatles," and featured Tony Sheridan as the lead singer.

The Beatles's first engagement, after returning from Hamburg, was at the Litherland Town Hall in England. The English fans noted the improvement in the group and began to respond to them enthusiastically. From then on, they had a devoted following.

[10]Ibid., p. 87.

During 1961, the Beatles played several large
ballroom dates in Liverpool. The group ~~was beginning to~~ *now*
realize the effect it had on audiences and made the most
of it. They were now in demand both in Liverpool and
Germany. The Beatles left England ~~in 1961 to~~ *and* return *ed* to
Hamburg. ~~It was at this time that~~ a German friend,
Astrid, told Stu that she didn't like his Teddy-boy hair
style. She restyled his hair, brushing it all down and
forward. "Stu turned up at the Top Ten that evening with
his hair in the new style, and the others collapsed on the
floor with hysterics." Two night later, "George turned up
with the same style. Then Paul had a go. . . . The Beatle
hair style had been born."[11]

When the Beatles returned home ~~from Hamburg~~ this
time, Stu Sutcliffe stayed behind. He chose to remain in
Hamburg to study art. Paul took over the bass guitar after
Stu left. Stu died less than a year later in Hamburg of a
brain hemorrhage.

[11]Ibid., p. 116.

The Big Break

The most important singular event in the development

of the Beatles took place

> . . . .on the afternoon of October 28, 1961. A youth . . .
> walked into the Nems record store in Whitehall,
> Liverpool, and asked for a record called "My Bonnie"
> by a group called the Beatles. Brian Epstein, who was
> behind the counter, said he was terribly sorry. He'd
> never heard of that record, or of a group called the
> Beatles.[12]

Brian was naturally curious, so in November, he went

to the Cavern, a club in Liverpool, to see the Beatles

perform. He was so fascinated by them that he began

asking questions about how one would go about managing

a group. Brian, now 27 and independently wealthy, was

becoming bored with selling records. After repeated visits

to the Cavern, he decided to make the Beatles his new

hobby.

Brian arranged an informal meeting with the Beatles in

December. The boys decided to give him a try as their

manager. Brian immediately set up a company for the

Beatles called Nems Enterprises. He tool over all of the

bookings and ingeneral, organized the business area

[12]Ibid., p. 127.

completely and efficiently. He advised the Beatles on how to act, how to dress, and how to talk both on and off stage.

Since Brian was the owner of one of the most successful record stores in England, he had many contacts already established with the major recording companies. He approached Decca Records first with his new find. Decca promptly turned down the Beatles ~~proclaiming them~~ a *saying they were* bad risk. He did, however, manage to sign the Beatles with Electric and Musical Industries Ltd., shortly after the refusal from Decca. EMI is the largest recording organization in the world.

.An EMI executive suggested the removal of Pete Best *Since* ~~as~~ he considered Pete the least talented and most difficult to work with. Ringo Starr (Richard Starkey) was chosen to replace Pete as the group's drummer.

Stardom

On September 11, 1962, the Beatles recorded their first
disc on EMI's Parlophone label. It was called "Love Me
Do."[13] Only 100,000 copies were sold. But it marked
The last time a Beatle record would sell less than a half-
million copies. "Love Me Do" was followed by "Please,
Please Me," which hit the number one spot on the British
charts.

> . . . the third, "From Me To You," also made number
> one (louder), and the fourth, "She Loves You," made
> the biggest hit that any British artist had ever cut. All
> of them were written by Lennon and McCartney.[14]

By 1963, Beatlemania had spread across the entire
British Isles and reached America the following year.

The first Beatle record release in America was "I
want to Hold Your Hand." Ten days before the record
was issued for sale, one million copies had been ordered.
The Beatles was only a name on a record in America at
this time.

The Beatles ~~were introduced in person~~ came to the American

[handwritten marginal note: See note on page 12. You first said "Beatlemania had reached America."]

[13]Capitol Records Biography, March 1968.

[14]Nik Cohn, Rock (New York: Pocket Books,
1969), p. 116.

~~public~~ in February, 1964. Prior to their arrival, the largest

craash publicity program in history was launched by

Brian Epstein. The Beatles were nervous about the

reception awaiting them in America. So far, none of their

records had reached the number one position on the

American charts. As soon as they arrived at Kennedy

Airport, their fears were over. They were greeted by

10,000 screaming fans. Airport officials said of that day,

"Incredible. We've never seen anything like this before,

not even for kings and queens!"[15]   Top Forty radio

stations were recording time in Beatle minutes. The

temperature was given in Beatle degrees.

"I Want to Hold Your Hand" was in the number 45

position on the American pop charts. After the arrival of

the Beatles, it zoomed to number one in two weeks. It was

marked as one of the fastest selling records in the history

of show business.

> By the beginning of April, there were twelve Beatle
> records on the list of the 100 best sellers in the country,
> and, astonishingly, five of these held the top five
> positions. . . . Overwhelmed by this activity, the music
> industry estimated that the Beatles records actually
> accounted for 60 per cent of the entire singles

[15]Jerry Hopkins, The Rock Story (New York: The
New American Library, 1970), p. 70.

[Handwritten margin note: Oup.!! you said a million copies had been ordered. And this song was in 45th spot on the charts?]

business during the first three months of 1964.[16]

The Beatles spent the next two years touring all over the world. They had a hectic schedule which left little time for their creative development. George Harrison said of those years:

> We got in a rut, going around the world. It was a
> different andience each day, but we were doing the
> same things. There was no satisfaction in it. Nobody
> could hear. It was just a bloody row. We got worse as
> musicians, playing the same old junk every day. There
> was no satisfaction at all.[17]

Breaking all show business records was a common occurrence during the Beatle tours. In Kansas City, for example, a local rock show promoter offered Brian $100,000 for the Beatles to do a show. Brian declined the offer saying that the Beatles needed a day of rest. The promoter tore up the check and wrote one for $150,000. Brian checked with the Beatles themselves on this offer. They were playing cards when he approached them about the $150,000. Without looking up from their game, they told Brian it was up to him. Brian

[16]Carl Belz, The Story of Rock (New York: Oxford University Press, 1969), p. 130.

[17]Davies, p. 214.

accepted the offer for the prestige value. It was the

highest fee ever paid for a single performance in the

history of show business.

On the Beatles third tour of America, the attendance at

Shea Stadium in New York on August 23, 1966, was over

55,000. The show grossed the highest receipts in show

business history~~,~~ *, and* The Beatles broke their former

"highest fee paid" record ~~at Shea Stadium~~ *the Shea Stadium*. They

received $189,000 for that performance.[18] The

Beatles played their last concert ~~on this tour. It was~~

~~given~~ in San Francisco, California, on August 29,

1966.

[18]Norris and Ross McWhirter, eds., <u>Guinness</u> <u>Book</u> <u>of</u>
<u>World</u> <u>Records</u> (New York: Bantam Books, 1970),
p. 189.

A Fateful Decision

Chapter heading
p. 1.
see

The Beatles decision to end touring was based on their

claim that their music had developed to such a degree

and employed so many electronic devices, that it was no

longer possible to create the effect in concert.

Brian Epstein was greatly saddened by the Beatles'

decision to end touring. For him, it meant little

Who said?

involvement with the affairs of the Beatles. Brian was said

to be frustrated creatively and that he lived out his own

dreams through the reality of the Beatles.

In 1967, Brian died at the age of 33. His death was

ruled accidental by a coroner's court on September 8,

1967.

Brian's death marks the end of t he financially

successful era of the Beatles. Although the creative genius

of the Lennon-McCartney team was more prolific and

more unusual after Brian's death, the Beatles, as a

commercial rock group never fully recovered from the

blow. Quarrels among the Beatles were frequent and the

subject was usually money.

Chapter heading
see p. 1.

Their Music

During these difficult times, they turned out some of the best compositions that the world of modern pop music has ever known.

Their first major accomplishment was an album called "Sergeant Pepper's Lonely Hearts Club Band." It was released in 1967.

double space

In musical substance, there are many musical structures in "Sgt. Pepper's" that are both new and extremely interesting, as well as new chord progressions, new instrumentations, and a continuation of the great fresh flow of melody. "A Day in the Life" is not only the most ambitious thing they ever wrote but possibly the best piece of music they've done up to now.[19]

double space

After "Sergeant Pepper" came "Magical Mystery Tour." It contained six new, distinctively different compositions.

Magical Mystery Tour, opens with a string backbeat, but this is merely a conceit; it offers no musical indication of what is to follow. In fact, the six new songs on this album represent six distinct styles.[20]

double space

[19]"Sgt. Pepper," New Yorker, June 24, 1967, p. 22.

[20]Edward Davis, ed., The Beatles Book (New York: Cowles Education Corporation, 1968), p. 133.

The Beatles released "Abbey Road" in September 1969. In my opinion, "Abbey Road" is the finest production of all. From "Here Comes the Sun" to "Maxwell's Silver Hammer," it is a recording of musical genious.

> Shimmering brilliance and unbounded creative energy grace every moment of "Abbey Road." It is alternately bright, silly, warm, funny, childlike, funky, and glib. . . .
> If side one is the study in contrasts, side two is the ultimate in total blending and rhythmic balance. It is the sun side, suffused with mellowed warmth woven together with motifs, bridging, reprises, surprises, with all the songs set within one another.[21]

The Beatles released two more albums after "Abbey Road." They were "Hey Jude" and "Let It Be." Before "Let It Be" was released to the public, Paul McCartney announced his was separating from the group to pursue his own career. Paul said that he enjoyed his family more than the Beatles and preferred to spend more time with his wife and daughters. The truth was that quarrels had become more frequent. Apple Corps. Ltd, a corporation which the Beatles founded after Brian Epstein's death had

[21]Ellen Sander, "The Beatles: Abbey Road," Saturday Review, October 25, 1969, p. 69.

failed miserably. They made many mistakes without

Brian's watchful eye. The feud between John and Paul

grew steadily. Their personality opposites had once

been an asset in their creative projects. Where John was

the cynic, Paul was the dreamer. They checked and

complimented one another. Now, the relationship had

reached the breaking point.

> With the millions rolling in and rolling out again like
> bilge on a sinking ship, John persuaded Paul to hand
> the checkbook over to Allen Klein, . . . a man Paul
> found offensive. Chagrined, Paul retreated to a farm in
> Scotland, where he watched Klein prune the Apple. . . .[22]

Paul, almost immediately after his announcement of

the break-up, released an album of his own. It was simply

called "McCartney," and is exactly that—all McCartney.

Paul wrote every song, composed all the music, played

every instrument, and sang all the parts. His wife, Linda,

handled the photography for the album jacket. "Overall,

the new album is good . . . but it is nothing to match his

past pop classics. . . ."[23]

[22]"The Beatles Decide to Let It Be--Apart,"
Life, April 24, 1970, p. 39.

[23]"Hello, Goodbye, Hello," Time, April 20,
1970, p. 57.

Conclusion

Chapter heading see p. 1.

It is difficult to imagine that the Beatles could have gone on indefinitely producing distinctively creative material. But, is it possible they can do it ~~alone~~ *individually*? It is doubtful. John released an album that was ~~he~~ *he* recorded in Canada. It was a complete failure. Even the reports of the McCartney "death" couldn't boost the sales of Paul's album to even bring it near the sales marks set by earlier Beatle albums.

The Beatles strove all through their career together, to find an identity individually. John wrote his books. His first, In His Own Write, reached the best-seller list almost as soon as it was off the press. It is now in its 15th printing. But it was Paul who suggested the title.

John? Or you need to make a stronger transition from John to Paul.

Ringo, who didn't often get into the songwriting act, although he is the one who wrote "Octapus' Garden," decided to set his sights for acting.

George was always more interested in mysticism and lacked active involvement in the later years of the Beatles. He had written a number of songs the group recorded.

John, in my opinion, needs the help of Paul in his *See P. 17* creative output, musically anyway. His music is too harsh

and stark without Paul there to tone it down. Paul's solo

music lacks the strength of his former compositions which

included the collaboration of John.

Seeing and hearing the Beatles individually now, lends

insight to the Beatles as a group. The talent was and is

inherent. But each segment of it is powerless without its

counterpart.

***

BIBLIOGRAPHY

Aronowitz, A.G. "Wisdom of Their Years." Life, (January 31, 1969), p. 12.

"The Beatles." Capitol Records Biography, (March 1968), pp. 1-10.

Inconsistent information with FN 1 and 13.

"The Beatles Decide to Let It Be–Apart." Life, (April 24, 1970), p. 39.

Belz, Carl. The Story of Rock. New York: Oxford University Press, 1969.

Coffin, P. "Art Beat of the '60's." Look, (January 9, 1968), pp. 32-41.

Cohn, Nik. Rock. New York: Pocket Books, 1969.

Davies, Hunter. The Beatles, The Authorized Biography. New York: Dell Publishing Co., Inc., 1968.

Davis, Edward, ed. The Beatles Book. New York: Cowles Education Corporation, 1968.

Fager, C.E. "Apple Corps. Four." Christian Century, (March 19, 1969), pp. 386-8.

a good bibliography

"Hello, Goodbye, Hello." Time, (April 20, 1970), p. 57.

Hildreth, Peter. Name-Dropper. London: McWhirter Publishing Company Limited, 1970.

Hopkins, Jerry. The Rock Story. New York: New American Library, 1970.

Jahn, M. "After Sgt. Pepper; Magical Mystery Tour Album." Saturday Review, (December 30, 1967), p. 55.

Kroll, J. "It's Getting Better." Newsweek, (June 26, 1967), p. 70.

McWhirter, Norris and Ross, eds. Guinness Book of World Records. New York: Bantam Books, 1970.

Sander, Ellen. "The Beatles: Abbey Road." Saturday Review, (October 25, 1969), p. 69.

"Sgt. Pepper." New Yorker, (June 24, 1967), p. 22.

Zimmerman, P. D. "Inside Beatles." Newsweek, (September 30, 1968), p. 106.

Sound research technique is evident in your paper, both in the bibliography and the excellent quotations.

Your basic question is: Why are the Beatles successful? Did Epstein's promotional abilities do it? Or is it the Beatles' inherent talent? You wrestled with this question but didn't resolve it.

Perhaps "successful" is too vague. Do you mean commercial success or artistic success? Which success did you have in mind in the introduction?

Mechanically, the paper needs revision and closer attention to final copy preparation. Cut unnecessary words and rearrange word and sentence order. Avoid typographical errors.

It's a good paper. Thank you.

Index

NOTES